CW01083564

NO ONE'S LOSER

No One's Loser

HOW I MASTERED THE LAW OF ATTRACTION AND YOU CAN, TOO

Jess Williams

Copyright © 2023 by Jess Williams

The information provided in this book is for educational and informational purposes only. It is not intended to replace professional advice or treatment. The author and publisher are not liable for any damages or negative consequences resulting from any information or suggestions contained in this book. Readers should always seek the advice of a qualified professional before making any changes to their health, lifestyle, or behavior. The reader assumes full responsibility for any actions taken based on the information provided in this book.

All rights reserved. No part of this book may be reproduced in any manner whatsoever without written permission except in the case of brief quotations embodied in critical articles and reviews.

First Printing, 2023

To my Grandmother Jessie, my namesake. Thank you for loving me unconditionally. For allowing me the freedom to be creative and for cultivating this gift. For challenging me to push towards greatness, even when I resisted. For teaching me to walk by faith. You knew it all along. I love you. I miss you. I know you're proud.

Contents

Introduction

"Our deepest fear is not that we are inadequate. Our deepest fear is that we are powerful beyond measure. It is our light, not our darkness, that most frightens us. We ask ourselves, 'Who am I to be brilliant, gorgeous, talented, fabulous?' Actually, who are you not to be?"

—Marianne Williamson

Whether you believe in God, the universe, or any higher power, you should know undoubtedly that the powers that be are great at giving you exactly what you ask for, and this is by very meticulous and intentional design. *"Ask, and it shall be given to you."* This knowledge dates back centuries. Long before any of us were conceived. Many philosophies, from ancient Proverbs to some of the world's greatest innovators such as Henry Ford or Albert Einstein, all have the same theory; what you think, you always become and that couldn't be more true. However, there is a science or formula behind this concept that the world's most successful individuals have mastered. A formula that has been kept from the likes of you and me for far too long.

When I discovered the Law of Attraction through the teachings of authors like Charles F. Haanel, Chin-Ning Chu, Rhonda Byrne, Sun Tzu, Jim Rohn, and many, many more, I wondered why more people weren't taking advantage of the great source of power at their fingertips. The answer is simple. Most of us lack the discipline we need to reach our true potential, and others simply don't believe that it can work for them. Before I read my first book on the topic, you couldn't have paid me to believe it. An unseen force is noting what I focus my energy on and sending more of that my way? I'd call you crazy and charge it to me just being unfortunate.

It wasn't until I took the first step towards finding my truth, figuring out who I am and what my purpose is, that I began to see for myself just how powerful we are. Utilizing this power is far beyond simply reading a book cover to cover. After finishing many of these pieces of literature I felt excited for my newfound superpower. I went to sleep with a plethora of gratitude and woke up the next day ready to test the might of this power surging through me.

Initially, and to my surprise, nothing changed. I was appalled the world around me was remaining the same. What gall. *How dare you keep me from being great! I can't possibly be doing anything wrong. I read the entire book!*

It wasn't the fault of these teachings, it was me. Under the surface I still had things to work out that these books could not make magically disappear. The authors of these works came from a very different time than I did and a lot had changed. I thought I could force everything around me to do the work for me. Through much trial and error, I realized the problem remained with my subconscious thought and my response to the world around me. I found myself following the practices I had learned for a few days then reverting back to my old habits. I couldn't paint the things I didn't like pink and think I would dislike them less. They were what they are, just in pink. I had to want to *truly* change before I would see results.

Your subconscious mind is like a whisper in the wind. There is an old question we've all heard at least once. If a tree falls in a forest and no one is around, does it make a sound? The answer is *YES.* You wonder if because it cannot be heard, it never happened. But it did. Just because you aren't saying it out loud doesn't mean it isn't flowing into the realm of your existence. In fact, your obsessive, subconscious thoughts are more potent than thinking aloud, and they are happening even when you aren't aware.

Take a moment right now to capture your current thoughts. You aren't focused. You might be thinking about bills, loved ones, problems that shouldn't matter at this moment. It happens. You're only human. Don't attempt to control these thoughts at this moment. It will become a fight and your mind will win. You are mindful that they are happening. Now, bring your attention back to the present moment. Together we will work on breaking these chains and creating dominant, positive thought patterns and behaviors that will gradually change you. That's right. YOU. We often think the key to a better life is attempting to force the things around us to change; to fight to control everything but our behaviors and thoughts. True change will always begin from within. Everything else will march to the rhythm of the beat you drum.

Often, perfectly imperfect humans that we are, the hardest person to love is you. You feel as though you don't deserve it. You often compare where you are in life to society's idea of who you should be. You follow unrealistic timelines of when you should be married, when you should start having children, or when you should be the CEO of that successful company you built from the ground up. That's a lot of pressure for one person simply trying to find their way in life. Let's be real, deadlines for projects are significant, but deadlines in life don't always work out the way you think they will, and you should always be prepared to navigate this uncertainty, but never give up on what you truly desire.

Instead, create milestones that place you closer to your goals, conditioning you each step of the way. These small triumphs will lead you to significant victories. It's easier to build on a foundation made of solid concrete than sand. Focus precisely on what you dream of happening for you, have faith that it will all work out as long as you intend for it to and keep your end of the deal by putting in the work that needs to be done. When you spend too much time stressing about how you'll be a millionaire or how you'll snag that dream job, you lose non-refundable time which could have been spent working towards reaching those milestones and setting the intention that you are ready to receive. Moreover, worrying about how these big dreams of yours will become your reality is stressful work that no one will benefit from. You must learn to set your intentions and let the universe worry about the heavy lifting, but understand that this does not mean you are to sit and wait for results; there is still plenty of room for your own will to be done. There is no such thing as the perfect time to "start" working on yourself or your goals. Tomorrow is not promised. What matters most is what you can do today. The time is always *now*. In a world where everyone claims to be real, it's finally time to be *real* with yourself.

This book is not intended to be your typical self-help, secret-to-success guide. I won't create fantasies for you or sell you any magic beans. I will simply share with you, my truth. For these methods to work, YOU have to work. Tell yourself you have what it takes, and no one can take that away from you, not even you. I'm here to give you the tough love and that extra push you may need. I have been where you are on my journey. I understand that it isn't always as easy to keep pushing as it is to give up and pretend it wasn't that important. I've taken a leap of faith that by being vulnerable and sharing these experiences, I will be the messenger for anyone ready to receive the message. The fountain of knowledge is ever-flowing, and I encourage and challenge YOU, like me, to continue to drink from it even after you've finished this book. Knowledge is the truest form of power. Knowledge frees you from fear. Take a moment to set your intentions. Now take a deep breath and hold it for three seconds. Exhale. Repeat once more if need be. Shall we begin?

1

The Story of Me Part I

I was always a unique child, so says my mother. From what I remember of my childhood, growing up in South Central, Los Angeles, I had a particular curiosity about how things worked. A real passion for learning and exploration. I was the kid that would take something apart just to rebuild it or get creative and design doll clothes from old socks because we couldn't afford to buy them. I would also sometimes get in trouble for this very act. Sorry about your cassette player, Sis.

My beautiful mother, Yolanda, told me I could read as young as age two, and I recall writing vivid short stories as early as kindergarten. My loving, late Grandmother, Jessie, helped my mother raise my sister and I in our humble one-bedroom home in South Central and worked at my elementary school as administrative secretary to our principal. She was a hardworking, well respected, God-fearing woman with many incredible talents of her own. She had the most beautiful, big, bright smile with the deepest dimples. And even in her 50s, she could salsa in six-inch heels with the best of them. I think we were more afraid of seeing "Ms. Jessie" over the principal when we got into trouble at school. She was someone you always wanted to impress. Someone unafraid to give you equal parts of unconditional love and *what you need to hear, but might not want to*. She was also one of the primary motivators for me becoming my best self, indeed, my biggest source of support. When she noticed how advanced I was, she ensured that I continued to have opportunities to strengthen my newfound "gift", even when I, a young kid who obviously knew what was best for me, didn't want to comply.

I remember the time she enlisted my talents in our school district's poetry contest. I had to have been in at least 1st or 2nd grade. I had no idea who Langston Hughes was, but apparently, it was a big deal for me to recite one of his poems in front of a bunch of strangers. I was always pretty timid, but even as a child, I had a special gift of the gab that helped me maneuver many things in my favor.

One of the teachers, Mrs. Ross, was in charge of getting our school's participants ready for the big day. I convinced her to barter with me. If I participated, I'd choose any toy from the big bag of toys she kept in her classroom. Children of all grades across the school could only dream of digging into this bag of treasure. She agreed, and the deal was set. Every day after school, I'd rush to her classroom and practice my poem with only one thing in mind. Which toy would I take home? I would even recite it to my mother and grandmother at home.

Before I knew it, the big night was upon us. That toy was mine! My mother dressed me in my Sunday best, and when it was my turn, I stood and walked to the head of the room. I never liked large crowds or too much attention. There, with my mouth gaped, all of Langston's beautiful words filled the room. By the time I was finished, I had received a standing ovation.

Ultimately, I went on to lose the competition. The winner, ironically, was the child of someone who was in a high position of power within our school district. Ahh, my first taste of nepotism. Though I hadn't initially wanted to participate, I was still a bit upset. I felt robbed! It was no longer about the toy, but my desire to win. Without my realization, that became the real prize. My family gave me a lot of love and support. They were letting me know that I still did a great job.

This was my first real experience of losing. It was at that moment that I decided I would be no one's loser. This moment lit a fire I never knew existed. I was able to pick my treasure from the big bag of goodies anyway, but it didn't feel the same. I yearned for more.

2

You Want It, You Got It

"I could not, at any age, be content to take my place
by the fireside and simply look on. Life was meant to
be lived. Curiosity must be kept alive. One must never,
for whatever reason, turn his back on life."

— **Eleanor Roosevelt**

* * *

As a child, I was pretty good at figuring out ways to get what I wanted (most of the time). My mother and grandmother both worked very hard, full-time, to ensure my sister and I had the necessities. Their main priority was a good education, so for much of my grade school years we attended the local private Catholic schools, which certainly weren't cheap. As an adult I now understand that this, on top of monthly bills, personal debt, and other expenses, is why I didn't always get the latest Nikes or that bright yellow electric scooter I saw in the mall at Christmas, but what kid thinks about these things? I didn't!

Early on, I figured out ways to get the material things I wanted. I was too scared of Grandma to steal (and I hear it's not a very good thing to do), so I had to come up with other means. A job? *No way*! I barely liked doing my homework, and who would hire a kid? Perhaps an allowance? Yeah, right! Those Happy Meals I asked for always turned into "we have food at the house" meals. There was no way I was getting money just because.

I heard that bartering began around 8000 years ago in Mesopotamia, when tribes needed to negotiate to get hold of the spices, weapons, and other items they needed. Well in the 90s I worked out that it was a good way to get what I wanted, too.

Using my "gift of gab," I was able to barter with the neighborhood kids or kids at my school for things that I wanted, which was always toys or video games. I was able to convince them that whatever "beloved" item I had was something they needed, and we should trade-off. Using this method, I was able to acquire a few of the things my mother couldn't afford to get me. When she questioned the origin of these random toys that were popping up around the house, I was able to talk my way out of trouble (most of the time). My case was so convincing they were sure I'd grow up to become a lawyer.

Think of all of the things that you want in life. This does not solely have to be material possessions. In a sense, the act of manifestation and the Law of Attraction is your way, as an adult, of bartering with the universe. There are things you want from the universe, and there are things the universe needs from you in return. Showing gratitude for all that you have today and maintaining a genuine spirit of giving are essential practices that will lead the universe to reciprocate your vibration. Because of this, you must always be prepared to receive and be mindful of what frequencies you put out. The powers that be do not discriminate. It does not know the difference between what you may or may not want. All it knows is what you think, what you speak, and what you feel. It doesn't care if you are poor or rich, Black, White, Democrat or Republican. The only things that matter are the frequencies you put into the world and the vibrations it responds with, and it will *always* respond.

So how do you get the universe to respond in the way that you want? Don't "fake the funk." You have to feel a real sense of gratitude and dispel every morsel of negativity that you can. This means negative thoughts, negative people, and negative behaviors. Gratitude is not a one-off action that you can quit practicing once you get your way.

As humans, we often find ourselves being most thankful *after* we receive a blessing or only praying when we want something good to happen, just to denounce all faith if it doesn't go our way. This produces the energy of desperation and will continue to re-cycle situations that cause feelings of lack and need in your life. You have to condition yourself to be consistently grateful for even the smallest bit of good. This practice will make the act of gratitude a more natural and powerful occurrence. Before you know it, the universe will be conditioned to respond to those vibrations without you even realizing it. You will also begin to feel happier, more present, optimistic and energetic. There is something to be grateful for every day. You can start with the fact that you are blessed to see that day.

There are people in the world that do not believe they deserve any good. We all know someone like this. It may very well be you who feels this way. We see someone doing well, and we envy them or covet the things that they have. We try to figure out how to get what they have or better. We want to "one-up" them or compete. We wonder why them over us. When someone wins the lottery or finds money on the ground, we say to ourselves, "that would never happen to me!" And guess what? As far as the universe is concerned, you're right! Whatever you think of yourself, you are. So why let mentally crippling thoughts of self-doubt poison the same fountain from which you drink? We are indeed our own worst enemy at times.

Instead of dwelling on the things I didn't want, I replaced those thoughts with thoughts of things I *did* want to happen. I set my intentions and spared no specifics to detail, thanked the universe for it and let it do its job figuring how it will find its way to me. Stop telling yourself you're tired of being alone. Instead tell yourself you are thankful for the time you get to spend with yourself and cannot wait to share special moments with someone that is perfect for you. Take that time to get to know *you* better. Instead of complaining about your *need* for more money, (because the universe will respond with more need), replace those thoughts with happiness for having more than enough money now and more money is on its way to you. If you have to chase it, it will run, but if you're patient, it will come.

The universe can respond in the smallest or most grand way, and this is up to your thoughts and actions. You can't say that you want a better life for yourself and then do everything that is the exact opposite. What you think, feel, and do have to be in total sync. In many cases, this task is easier said than done, which is why self-discipline is essential. It will also be in your best interest to focus on major accomplishments individually. Afterall, you don't see any heart surgeons that are also astronauts. How many lives can they save from space? By spreading yourself too thin, you're not letting those good nutrients get to the places they're needed most. Remember, the world's most beautiful buildings, some of which have stood for much longer than many of us, were built one brick at a time.

Take a moment to think of something small that you've asked the universe for. It can be something as simple as a parking spot in a busy shopping center or winning a raffle. How many times have you been "lucky" enough to find the last shirt or pair of shoes that you were looking for, just before you gave up, and it just so happens to be in your size? How many times has someone come to mind, and they end up calling you, or you see them out in public? The first thing you say to them out of excitement is, "I was just thinking about you!" This is no coincidence. At that moment, you willed some potent frequencies and subconsciously doubled-down on receiving. This happened through visualization and feelings of gratitude and happiness without you even knowing. How many times did you say "thank you" in your mind or aloud? You probably visualized yourself in those shoes or that shirt. You thought of what you'd do and how you'd feel after winning that raffle. Feelings emerged when thinking about that person. According to the Law of Attraction, "like attracts like," which is why we also hear old sayings such as "misery loves company," because that's true too.

I remember the times in school I didn't want to be called upon during a lesson, and I did everything in my power not to be called on. Well, at least I thought I did. Instead, I was drawing more attention to myself by sinking lower into my seat or making an uncomfortable face that I thought translated to "not me, please not me," only to be *the chosen one*. My entire focus was on not being picked only to still be picked. This was a form of call and response between myself and the universe. Think of the many young artists that have created songs where they speak misfortune or death into their life. Or the same ill intent they wish for their enemy is claimed as their own fate? How many of those same artists' lives have been lost to some unfortunate event? We underestimate the power of the mind and tongue.

When I got into the workforce and was always selected for special projects over other employees, I often felt as though I was being singled out for extra work because I was so outspoken. Then I realized I had willed many of these opportunities due to my work ethic. It was evident I was the most reliable and the most prepared to do the job the way it needed to be done. But this isn't something I understood until I looked at the situation in retrospect.

For a long time, I was simply there to do a job (sometimes at the bare minimum) and collect my check. But the longer I did the job, the better I got at it, and the more invested I became. For me, this was a blessing in disguise because I ended up being promoted multiple times over the course of a year. I increased my influence in the workplace significantly, as well as earning an exponential increase in my salary. And though I had more responsibilities, in a sense, I also gained more freedom to navigate my work day however I chose. You are waiting to receive everything good you want from the universe, and it will respond when you are ready. Your plane is caught in turbulence and it is up to you to find it somewhere safe to land.

3

The Story of Me Part II

My grandmother continued to bet on her "Pooh Bear." Her gift was the gift of song. She was an incredibly talented singer and part of a well known local gospel group called the Los Angeles Gospel Jewels. They frequently traveled the country, singing their hearts out at various conventions and events, even appearing with notable artists like Al Green, Shirley Caesar, and The Mighty Clouds of Joy, to name a few. Testing the waters, my grandmother got me involved with our school choir. I had no idea if I could sing or not, but I did it anyway. For an elementary school choir, we were a force to be reckoned with. We went on to win many competitions. I sang soprano, like my grandmother.

By age nine, my love for music had grown so vast there was never a moment that I wasn't singing or writing songs. My grandmother had an old tape recorder my sister would use to play her cassette mixtapes. She'd record her favorite records from the radio and play them back. I knew I wasn't supposed to listen to hardcore rap music at that age, but I did anyway, and I loved every bit of it.

Though my grandmother, sister, and I shared a room in our one-bedroom home in LA while my mother slept on the couch, she still allowed my sister to hang up all of her favorite hip hop posters. I remember seeing posters of Heavy D & The Boyz, Ras Kass, Immature, and Lil' Kim plastered on our cracked, pale blue walls. We even had matching New Kids On The Block comforter sets.

One day, "Little Me" had an idea. What if I took that old tape recorder and made my own songs? I could be just like the hip hop artists we listened to. People would have posters of *me* on their walls. This was the moment I decided that I would change the course of my life forever. I no longer wanted to be a paleontologist looking at old bones all day. Singing was what I loved to do. And like that, at age nine, I decided on my journey for decades to come. Boy, was I in for a ride.

I went on to record my first song ever. I laugh now when I think about how terrible it was, but at that moment, I felt like I deserved a Grammy or two. My sister wasn't too pleased when she found out I had dubbed my vocals over her favorite radio rips, and as revenge, she thought she'd teach me a lesson by sharing my hit song with all her teenage friends in our neighborhood.

Her plan backfired when her friends saw me sitting in my favorite spot on the porch one day and told me they'd heard my song. One of them even recited the lyrics. I didn't know any better then, they were probably doing it in jest, but instead of discouraging me, that was enough confirmation for me to keep at it. And I did. I wrote more, I recorded more, and I got better. My family noticed the change. They saw my passion. All I knew was that I enjoyed doing it. It made me happy. My grandmother enrolled me in UCLA's Young Writers Workshop one summer, and that was my tipping point.

Writing and creating music helped me build the confidence I needed to share my gift with the world. I never considered myself one of the "cool kids," but I got along with everyone I interacted with. And though I was still a bit shy, if you were lucky enough to get to know me, you'd quickly learn there was more than met the eye. I continued to be a student of my craft. And my grandmother ensured I knew not only the creative side but the business side of the music industry as well. She invited over friends that had seen the success I dreamt of reaching, to talk to me one-on-one and teach me the business. I dedicated myself to this dream, turned it into a new reality, and over time, it certainly began to pay off.

4

Discover Your Passion, Discover Yourself

"Knowing yourself is the beginning of all wisdom."
— **Aristotle**

* * *

I knew what I wanted at a very young age, and for several seasons, I was right. Many of the choices I made were strategic. Many were not. Not everyone discovers their life path at such an early stage. For most, it is not found until adulthood. For some, death comes before discovery. It's often overlooked how important it is to know what you want so you know where you're going, but one shouldn't rush to make this discovery. As long as you move forward, you'll never be left behind. It will come to you naturally. *Need only manifests more need.*

The flashing lights blind many of us. We see it on TV and social media all the time. We all want the beautiful dream home, a nice car, and a bank account that makes us smile just at its sight.

We want a sense of freedom and the feeling of constant joy. I, too, wanted just this until I realized my idea of success was made up of smoke and mirrors. I thought the real accomplishment was in the items I possessed, not the hard work I did to place me in a position to have these things, and because of this, I wasn't fully present mentally for some critical moments in my journey. I didn't understand the importance of mindfulness—the act of focusing your awareness on the present moment. Taking a moment to relish in how far you've come before worrying about how much further you have to go. These moments are now memories that I cannot attach a feeling to—to relive any happiness I may have felt.

It's okay to draw inspiration from what you see, but remember this: passion over possessions. When I see photos of someone somewhere tropical, I'm motivated to go on that dream vacation I've been putting off. It's only natural. I begin jotting down places to visit on my bucket list and when the ideal time to visit these places would be. I release vibrations of joy. I may even go as far as pricing hotels and flights. Then I revert my focus to the present moment and the work I am doing because I understand this will get me there and I'm motivated to work smarter.

We've all seen photos on social media of some seemingly wealthy individual smiling next to a dream car, or flaunting jewelry and money. Don't obsess over not having that or wanting that for yourself. Instead, smile because you are happy for them, whether you know them or not. You should try to feel even more inspired and excited about your journey and feel a genuine sense of gratitude in knowing that your season will come—and a sense of urgency to prepare yourself for that moment. Your passion will get you there. Don't waste another second watching others live when you could be living too. And never allow yourself to feel envious of others who are currently in their season of winning. Gratitude and jealousy are like water and oil. Think of your gratitude as water and jealousy or envy as oil. When you pour the two into a clear glass you will see the water sink to the bottom and the oil rest at the top.

When you neglect your passion and chase possessions, however, you will always feel unfulfilled. You will still want more possessions. You will always be in competition. This is why you hear successful people preaching about following your passion, and everything else will come. We talked about this in the introduction. YOU have to do the work. You must first plant the seeds to bear the fruit. However, it doesn't end when you plant the seeds. Seeds need to be tended. For example, when I discovered my "seed" of music, I tended to it by continuing to write and record. I participated in programs that helped me become a better writer. Becoming a better writer helped me become a better artist. Thus, helping me connect with more people through my music. The more others saw me take myself seriously, they also began to take me seriously. Through lots of trial and error, I weeded out any self-doubt, unhealthy habits and relationships and eventually was able to bear the fruits of my labor when my first season came. What seeds are you planting, and what are you doing to ensure a healthy growth?

Ask yourself this: Who are you? No, who are YOU, *really*? If someone you had never met before asked you to describe yourself in one sentence and that'd be the idea of who you are that they'd share with the world, what would you say? Would you be pretentious? Would you admit that you didn't know? Naturally, we want everyone to see the best version of ourselves, and that's perfectly fine. It's human nature to want to be accepted or praised. For many, appearance is everything. I was like that for a long time. To be "liked" by all, but at what cost? Most of the time we try to impress people that are probably on their journey of self-discovery, too. The real freedom comes from not concerning yourself with what people think of you or seeking approval that you don't really need.

By not being honest with ourselves, we miss fundamental opportunities for self-improvement. This is a habit we have to break. Once you've acknowledged who you are, you must then ask yourself who you want to be. This, to me, is the most critical step in uncovering your path. Take a moment to imagine your best version of yourself. What are some things that stand out about your physical appearance? What has changed for the better? How do you walk into a room of people? Do you exude confidence? Are you in love with yourself? Can you look in the mirror and genuinely smile at what you see without judgement? What excites you? Are you able to do this for a living? If so, what steps can you take to get there? If not, what's stopping you from doing so? Asking yourself these sorts of questions can help to peel back layers and discover your true self. It can also help blueprint some of the necessary steps to take to get there. Most of the time, the answer is right in front of you. Are you paying attention?

For a long time, material wealth meant the world to me. I won't lie and say that material possessions don't mean anything to me today because, like you, I too enjoy giving and receiving nice things, but they are nowhere near as important as they once were. I treat them as rewards or ways to commemorate reaching a major milestone instead of spoiling myself for doing nothing. Reaching milestones I've set for myself and seeing real success is far more rewarding than purchasing things that made me look successful before I had done anything worthwhile.

I'm guilty of doing it solely for a reaction—seeking gratification through people's response to my new car or my new shoes. But it was a made-up image of how well I was doing at a time when I was probably hurting the most. This is part of the growth that comes with being honest with yourself. It's also the hardest. There's a huge difference between staying positive during a storm and being in total denial of it, even as you stand in rain, drenched head to toe, holding an umbrella that has seen better days.

In the past, I would announce every move I made, sometimes before anything was set in stone because I was fooled into believing it wasn't happening if it wasn't shared publicly. I would rely on the response of people that were not invested in my health, wealth or happiness to gauge how well I was doing. Sometimes we care too much about what other people think. Even when most people's opinions aren't even their own but a mashup of things they have heard or seen from other people. I started to see that not everyone needed to know, or was happy to see that I was doing well. People took these announcements as an opportunity to discourage me, wish ill, or use me for their own self-interest.

Imagine the game of chess. The object is to outwit your opponent and checkmate their king, while also protecting your own. If every premature announcement you made on social media or in conversations with others was guiding your opponent closer to your king, would you continue doing it? It's vital to keep certain things to yourself to avoid any influence from the outside world. This influence can often create great doubt or lead you to doing something for everyone but yourself.

I get it. Sometimes we are so excited and want to shout it to the world, but remember, not everyone is on this journey with you. For the greater good of your sanity and purpose, sometimes you need to protect your energy from the world's influence. Some of the people that are closest to you can be a deterrent from you reaching success because they have not yet met their own. They don't understand why it's so important for you to become the best version of yourself because they have not yet reached that point—and likely don't feel as though they need improvement.

Change is uncomfortable. To be successful at it, you must condition yourself by consistently doing the groundwork necessary to make the things you want the things you have. Some people's toxicity is so deeply entrenched in their roots that not being that way seems like a foreign concept. They will curse you to hell and back before seeing things your way. Some people you'd think would be happy to see you win will only congratulate you halfheartedly. Some people will look at you crazy when you speak of topics like manifestation and vibrations. When we find those rare few that are on the same frequency we get excited that we've finally found someone that understands the power and beauty of it all.

Your friends and family should support you by default, right? We'd like to believe this is the unspoken standard of the way things should work, but that isn't always the way it turns out. In many cases our biggest opposition during our ascension can be those that are closest to us. I used to take this to the heart until I realized my friends and family aren't my demographic. You shouldn't have to sell the people closest to you on the idea of believing in you. If they want to support you, allow them to do so genuinely, not because they expect something in return. By focusing on their lack of support you waste energy that can be utilized on reaching the people that you resonate with the most. They are out there waiting for someone like you!

Ask yourself another question: What would you love to do for the rest of your life? And no, nothing isn't an answer. The easiest way to get nothing is to do nothing. There is something that exists within you that holds your interest more than anything else. Something that makes you smile and feel hopeful just at the thought of it. Something you've pictured yourself making millions of dollars from. Something that will give you the freedom you long for. Perhaps you have dreams and aspirations that you've pushed to the back of your mind because at some point you have believed they are unattainable. I am here to tell you now that you are wrong. Have no shame in your dreams for there is nothing in this world that is unattainable by you as long as you want it enough and work towards achieving it. Every successful person in the world had to start somewhere. The key to their success is the fact that they started and never quit.

Consistent belief in yourself and your passion is only conditioning the universe to place you exactly where you need to be throughout your journey at the exact moment you need to be there. This belief, or *faith*, places you on the same frequency as your success. Before you move on, take a moment to write down exactly how you'll create your lane by following your passion and spare no detail. The more vivid you are, the better blueprint the universe has to follow. And try to refrain from the lottery or bank robberies, as tempting as they are. The act of writing your life plans or goals out, also known as "scripting", will make it more clear how to achieve them. You don't want to chase money or material possessions blindly because it will only guarantee you having neither. Think of it as a roadmap and be prepared to pivot or "reroute" when necessary. At the end of this, write out how thankful you are for it all. Revisit this plan every day for 30 days, you don't have to spend any more than five to ten minutes. Feel the happiness you'll experience the moment it all comes to fruition and be grateful.

The Art of Exceptional Living by Jim Rohn taught me that you don't have to be the strongest, the smartest, or the most creative to reach success. To stand apart from the herd, all you need to do is ordinary things exceptionally well. Now if you are the smartest, the strongest and the most creative, and it is destined for you to do exceptional things then that will be your journey, but if you are not, don't count yourself out either. There is greatness within us all. Figuring it out is the fun part.

5

The Story of Me Part III

My grandparents had married and divorced by the time I was born, but I still had a very special bond with them both. My grandfather, Billy, was tough as nails, and always spoke his mind with no regard for sparing feelings, but he loved his family dearly and would do anything for us. I always took it as tough love. In fact, it was a combination of his tough love and my grandmother's much softer approach that helped mold me into the person I am today. I believe I inherited the best parts of those two.

My grandfather became very ill and passed away in October 2009. It broke me. I would see him every holiday growing up and talk to him over the phone every week. We would also stop by on Sundays after church for dinner. Both he and my grandmother were the greatest cooks. I remember sitting on his lap telling him how scruffy his beard was and him having a good laugh about it. When he transitioned I wished that I had I called him more just to chat. To learn more about his life growing up and what made him, him. We always think about these things when it's too late.

I was still trying to heal myself when two years after his passing I also lost my grandmother. She transitioned the day after Thanksgiving 2011. I was also the one that found her and had to muster the strength to attempt resuscitation while on the phone with 911 because everyone else that was home was too hysterical to try, and understandably so. By this time my mother had been living with MS for nearly a decade. Here I was at age 22, having lost two of the pillars in my life back to back. Who did I have to run to for insight or those much needed "talks" to vent about life? I considered my grandmother my best friend. There was nothing quite like my Grandmama and Granddaddy.

Even though I was the youngest, she left me in charge of everything. I suppose she knew I was the most capable of ensuring her wishes were followed. I was asked to speak at my grandmother's homegoing. *How in the hell do you expect me to do that?* I could barely go a day without crying. I didn't want to do it. I was scared. I was hurt. I was angry. But I knew I owed it to her. She deserved more than mere words, but I would sit down, pray and let the words find their way to the sheet of paper in front of me. How could I possibly sum up her greatness in a matter of minutes at that podium?

In tribute to her, I went on to write one of the best pieces I've ever written. And though I was choked up, I pushed through and spoke at her service. A lot of tears and applause followed. My speech, however, was not the most memorable moment at her homegoing to me. My aunt Nadine, who is a decorated public speaker, shared the most beautiful, *and necessary*, words soon after me. She shared great stories most of us had never heard before. She made us laugh, *and cry*. But it was when she took a moment to speak directly to my mother, sister and I about growing up that resonated the most. She noted that it was time to become the women my grandmother had prepared us to be. That we no longer had her here as a safeguard and it was time to step into our light and keep our now family of three strong and flourishing. I knew I didn't have my grandmother to lean on anymore and it hurt, even till this day. I also knew she was preparing us for this day even until her last breath. She kept a journal that she wrote in daily, and upon her passing, all of the pages went missing except for instructions she wrote on what to do and who to call when her time came. Till this day no one knows what happened to those pages and we searched everywhere.

The loss of my grandmother was the final straw for me, and with my aunt's words of encouragement embedded in my mind, I began to work towards change. I knew it wouldn't be an easy task, but I also knew it wasn't an impossible one either. I started to condition myself to be fearless, and honestly, whom should I fear with my two new guardian angels watching over me? I became more intentional with how I maneuvered in life and business. And more honest with not only myself, but those around me. I became less selfish.

We wish our parents and grandparents could live forever, but the reality is that they can't and neither can we. Life is so fragile that every moment you're blessed to be alive is an opportunity to do something meaningful. It was a new season for me—a noticeable difference in the me people once knew. She gave me the tools I needed to succeed, but it was always up to me to use them. I knew I could no longer make excuses about why I wasn't successful. I could no longer blame my environment or the people around me for not doing more for me than I could *and should* be doing for myself. I set out to make an impact on the world around me and haven't looked back since.

6

Breaking Bad

"Discipline is choosing between what you want now and
what you want most."
—**Abraham Lincoln**

* * *

According to author Charles Duhigg, habits are formed through a psychological pattern called a "habit loop." This process takes on three parts: the trigger that places your brain in automation causing the behavior, then there is the behavior itself and finally the reward, which helps you remember that "loop" in the future. This would explain why people who have a habit of biting their nails don't stop until someone mentions it or they snap back into reality and realize what they're doing. These people aren't aware of the action because the habit itself is on autopilot.

Many of our habits are ingrained as children which is why it's so difficult to break them in adulthood. This does not mean it isn't possible. The same way they are formed is the same way you can condition yourself to kick the habit and that is through repetition. Do more of the opposite and it will become second nature. Think of a child that is learning to ride a bike for the first time. How many times have they said they were scared? How many times did they fall and get a bruise? The pain eventually went away along with the fear of falling. This is because they kept trying and surely enough found their balance. Now they can ride that same bike with no hands. All that may be left now are the scars, the lessons learned, and knowing that they made it through. This is no different than whatever it is you seek to accomplish in life. The more you try, the better you get and you will eventually succeed. Ask yourself, what is the cost of quitting now? And what is the cost of continuing to push forward?

Generational habits are passed down in every family and they can be good or bad, that part is subjective. Whether you are born rich or poor, your ancestors have passed on generational influences that have finally made their way down to you. This could be in the form of finances, foods, attitudes or beliefs. If you grew up seeing your parents, and their parents, abusing alcohol, eating unhealthily, or mismanaging finances, there is a likelihood that you too may inherit the same behaviors, even without realizing you have. Fortunately for you, you now realize you have a choice to keep this behavior or relinquish it to the deep pits this generational hurt belongs in, for the sake of future generations.

Children emulate what they see. We often see videos on the interweb of young kids saying some of the darndest things. Some make us laugh and others make us wonder where the hell they learned that from. We may even hear their parents in the background asking where they learned that from. Children listen... a lot! They mimic the behaviors of the people they see. You have to be the first in your family to recognize this and ensure it's the *good* habits they learn and not the damaging ones. Critical lessons don't have to be firsthand experience or punishment. We have to denounce this toxic way of thinking—of letting the people we love fail or be hurt, if they will allow us to help them prevent it.

I learned at a young age that walking in the street was dangerous, and it didn't take me being struck by a car to do so. I took heed to the warnings given to me and that was enough for me. Exhibit positive generational influences that your future children can pass on to their children and so on. Teach them about healthy eating habits through example. Allow them to learn financial responsibility and the value of a dollar at a young age. Give them the tools they need to discover what it is that they love and support them while they do it. If they decide they no longer want to do that, support them while they figure it out. But this all starts with you. Allowing our children to suffer just to teach them a lesson will only teach them to think they deserve to suffer and they will surely pass this belief on.

The global population of the world is made up of less than 1% of millionaires. However, these millionaires own nearly half of the planet's trillion-dollar wealth. While we clearly have generational wealth being passed down, there are the chosen few that were just like you that yearned for more. They didn't allow generational hurt to consume them and with all odds against them, they achieved astronomical success.

Becoming some multi-millionaire may not be your dream and that's okay. Perhaps you want just enough to clear your debts, take care of your loved ones and be financially free, healthy and happy. You can start by matching the frequency of good fortune and financial freedom through practicing the habits of someone with these attributes. You don't have to become an accountant, but you do have to start by managing your finances better.

My partner and I use excel sheets that are formatted with codes to help us manage our finances. Most people dread checking their bank account, especially if they know they've been spending frivo-lously. The old saying goes, "the richer get richer," and this is true. Most wealthy individuals remain that way because they manage their money properly and also make their money work *for* them. They remain on the frequency of abundance. The fact is this: If you can't manage $1,000 in your bank account today, gaining a million tomorrow won't help. You won't manage it any better and you'll soon end up right back where you started, if not worse. In my experience, no one manages their money as well as someone with $30 left in their account on a Monday of their pay week. And I know because that was once me. I would stretch my dollar as far as it could go until payday hit and then it was back to my old cycle of habits, mismanaging my money.

It is much more convenient to continue our bad habits because we are used to them. We've become complacent. Change makes us uncomfortable. In fact, it's the uncertainty that keeps us from changing. Even the slightest difference in routine feels like an in-convenience. It may even give you anxiety. You mustn't be afraid of facing yourself. How many times has something new or out of your norm been introduced to you? And how many times have you said no before you said yes? If you ended up giving in and moving forward with it, how many times have you said to yourself, "That wasn't that bad"? Or "I actually enjoyed it."

Putting an end to bad habits also gives you a perspective on the people around you. When you change, the world around you changes, but for many it is very much the same. People may say you've changed and, for them, it may appear as a negative change. Perhaps now, you no longer act like them, think like them, or do the same things they do. This is a part of your growth. They're right. You have changed—for the better.

Out of good intentions you may try to teach people a new way of life that they can live if they put these teachings you share to practice. For some it will resonate and inspire, but for many it will not. This may weaken your bond because they simply don't see things the way that you do and that's fine. It's not their season yet. In some cases, they may never come around to the idea. Not everyone is a believer and I learned the hard way that you cannot take this personally. What's meant for you, is for you. You may want to share it with those closest to you, but the moment they resist, let them. Refocus on yourself, wish them happiness and blessings, and continue on your journey.

Let's make a pact. According to researchers, it takes about 66 days to form a new habit. That is 66 consecutive days dedicated to replacing what's bad for you with what's good for you. Think of the best version of yourself again. What does this version of you do differently? Is it healthier eating habits? Drinking more water? Not biting your nails, or reading a new book every week? Big or small, it doesn't matter. Take a moment to write down the habit you're going to break or foster and how you plan on doing so. If you find it difficult to completely change habits, think of ways you can adjust it with something that is good for you. I recommend a journal or notebook for this activity. Now sign and date the bottom of this paper. This is your agreement to not only the universe, but most importantly yourself. Take this agreement and place it somewhere you'll see it every day.

Starting today and for 66 days, work on positive reinforcement. For example, if your habit is immediately picking up your phone the moment you wake up, replace that with a routine that doesn't allow checking social media until after you've completed a set of tasks that align with your goals. At the end of each day, or in the heat of the moment, write down things that may have triggered the habit that day. This will make you more aware of what causes the habit to occur. Knowing this will help you pre-empt the habit when a typical trigger happens. Continue this activity one habit at a time for each bad habit you wish to rid yourself of or a good habit you wish to gain. Before you know it, you will be on the cusp of the best version of you.

7

The Story of Me Part IV

The loss of my grandparents affected me in a way I'd never imagine, especially losing my best friend, my grandmother. I was forced to become the matriarch of my immediate family whether I was ready or not. I began to take care of my mother and sister the same way she had done, often putting their needs before my own. By this time, my mother was living in Arizona, and my sister and I could no longer afford our townhouse we had shared while taking care of our grandmother up until she passed. I ended up in various temporary living situations while I attempted to find my footing and I continued to pursue my passion of creation--until I hit a brick wall.

I didn't realize I hadn't given myself the proper time to grieve and it began to affect me mentally and physically. I believed that by drowning myself in my work, I could trick my grief into disappearing. I often contemplated ending my tenure here on Earth, but the thought of abandoning my family and friends kept me from acting out these thoughts. I even ended up in the hospital because of a severe anxiety attack, which I swore was the end of me as I'd never experienced one before. I was diagnosed with anxiety disorder and placed on medication that honestly didn't make me feel any better so I refused to take it. Instead I decided I would face my demons head on.

One day I took to Facebook to go look at my Grandmother's page. I admired her photos, her posts, and smiled to myself. I went so deep in the rabbit hole that I came across a couple of posts she had written to me and they couldn't have come at a better moment. In these posts she spoke to me about trusting God and remembering how favored I am. She told me that no matter what my "right now" may look like, great things were in store for me. Ignore the background noise, focus on my craft, and do what I did best.

Recollecting the time, effort, and energy my grandmother put into my dreams, this moment was a huge reality check. Even in the midst of her transition she never once lost her faith and still only wanted the best for us. I snapped out of my woes and got serious about music again. I didn't worry about *how* I would harvest the fruits of this next season, but I told myself (and the universe) I *would*.

I started reading more, and journaling my thoughts. I became obsessed with my red notebook that I wrote all of my thoughts in. I still have it. In it I wrote positive affirmations that I regularly went back to read. I wrote out my life goals followed by a "thank you" after each sentence, something I learned from *The Secret*. Every time I opened this notebook, I felt a sense of excitement and blessings. My grandmother always wanted us to have a relationship with God and though I'm nowhere near super religious, I knew it was important that I, at the very least, spoke to him regularly.

I was very reserved with my appearance for a long time. No crazy piercings, and no colored hair. A friend of mine from high school was an aspiring hair stylist, so I'd pay her to do my hair every couple of months. For a long time she tried to convince me to add some color. Me being me, I was thinking, *No way! That's ghetto!* But after months of pressing the issue, I was finally convinced to add some color.

The year was 2014 and we settled on ombre green. There weren't very many young Black women with this hair color at the time and that's what made my choice unique. I knew I would stand out. The very day that I made this drastic change to my appearance and introduced the new me to the world I was contacted on Twitter about auditioning for a commercial. The irony behind this is that they had seen a video of a freestyle I'd recorded with a prominent hip-hop website. What made this even more bizarre was the fact that this video had been filmed several months before it was actually released, which just so happened to be the week these casting agents set out to find their next star. Everything seemed to be coming full circle.

However, I was still skeptical. I come from an era where business is conducted via email, in-person or over the phone, not through some social network. This was a time online where scammers were ever-present. One of the big scams during this period was saying "Celebrity Y" is filming a music video and is casting at this inflated rate of pay, all you have to do is x, y, z. My friend told me to see what it was about anyway, so I did. Even if thoughts of me being kidnapped by some crazed lunatic lingered in the back of my mind. I knew I wouldn't go alone and took the chance.

I found myself at Castaway Studios in Los Angeles, and having never auditioned for anything ever, I'll admit I was very intimidated. There were at least a hundred or more people in attendance when I arrived. Dancers were showing off their moves. I can't dance. I can do a mean robot, but I'm not flipping into a handstand and spinning on my head. I felt out of place in a room full of people that obviously did this a lot, but I had to catch myself. This was the new and improved me and I was here by design. I straightened my posture and garnered the confidence I have when I'm on stage performing. Here I was, a tall, slender Black girl with green hair, mesh football jersey, skinny jeans with a flannel tied around her waist, and her hat to the back. This was me, take it or leave it.

There were three of us in the room auditioning in front of the casting director and several other important-looking people. Each of us had a different talent on display. We were asked to slate, and I had to guess that meant telling them about me, and we proceeded to share our gift. I recited a rap I'd written that displayed not only my writing style, but my passion and they loved it. Becoming more comfortable I showed them the real me. Being a natural clown, I cracked a couple of jokes and got everyone to laugh. They began to pay special attention to me. After about 30 minutes we were all thanked for coming and escorted out. At that moment I told myself I would be selected for this commercial and no one could tell me any different.

By the time I made it home I had received a phone call from the casting director's assistant saying they loved me and would like me to come back the very next day for a second audition. I couldn't hold back my happiness and told them *thank you* and how excited I was. They went on to email a short script that I'd have to remember and I got to work. I memorized the entire piece before I went to sleep. I was too excited to sleep anyway.

I probably woke up before the sun the next day and we headed back to Castaway Studios. There were more people auditioning, a lot of new faces, but this time felt different. This was now familiar territory. The casting director noticed me and asked if I'd learned my part. I told her yes and she took me to a conference room where she asked me to recite it. After hearing my take on it, she gave me a couple of pro tips and allowed me to stay in the room, away from all of the noise, to practice more. A million different emotions rallied throughout my brain. I wished my grandmother could have been there with me.

When it was my turn to audition a second time I stepped into that room and recognized most of the faces there, but there were some that were new. I heard a blue-eyed gentleman in a suit mention to the woman and man sitting next to him, "This is the one I was telling you about." Alright Jess, it was showtime. I was asked to slate again and they began asking me questions about my background. They started to deep dive into the life of little old me and started to ask questions about my grandparents, an obviously very touchy subject. I remember telling the tale of them both and how they were lost. I tried so hard to not let it get to me, but I broke down in tears during my audition. I thought to myself, dammit Jess, you messed up. I apologized, but they told me I didn't have to and appreciated my vulnerability. That was the moment they realized I was more than just a kid auditioning for a commercial, but a real person with a real story that ironically fit the same narrative they were pushing. *Full circle.* We wrapped audition number two and they thanked me for coming again. I left knowing that I had given it my all and if it was meant for me, no one could stop that.

I was halfway home when I got another call. This time, what they told me next would change my life forever. I was informed that I'd got the role and what my rate of pay would be. I thought she must have made a mistake when she told me the different amounts I would be paid, and for what. This was absolutely insane to me. I wished my grandparents were around so I could call and tell them what just happened. The first audition for something I'd ever done, I landed. At this moment, I was so thankful for the blessing of this new season for me. Things were finally turning around. The work

I'd done was not in vain and my childhood dreams were coming true. This was my first taste of manifestation and with this new found power I continued to craft the world around me through my thoughts and actions.

My commercial went on to have over one million television impressions. It could be seen on major networks like MTV, BET, VH1, Revolt, Fuse and more. I could be heard on radio stations across the country—my face in magazines and on billboards. "Who is that green haired girl?" was asked more times than I could count. Because of this opportunity I was able to travel and advocate for health and safety while sharing my story. I was still giving while receiving. I was afforded a chance to speak at the historical Howard Theatre in Washington D.C. in front of various stakeholders, publications, and congressmen and women. I was even offered a visit to the White House by an official. I was able to take this opportunity and create others for myself. This gave me a new rush of adrenaline. I fell in love with what I was doing again and knew my grandparents would be proud.

8

The Beginning of the Beginning

"Someone's sitting in the shade today because someone
planted a tree a long time ago."
—Warren Buffett

* * *

Every day is a new opportunity to make more progress than the day before. In fact, each day you work on yourself and your goals, you're closing the gap between you and whatever it is you wish to attain. With this in mind, each day should count. You are here for a reason and the moment you understand your purpose, the more conscious you become about how your time is spent, because unlike money, time is not refundable. Ask any successful individual who has accumulated wealth and accolades what they value most and they will all tell you the same answer: time. No one is asking you to be the next Gandhi, but know that before you leave this earth, be it big or small, you will leave an imprint. This is called your legacy. Now how do you want to be remembered?

Set your intention for your day the moment you wake up. Yes, this means before you pick up your phone and scroll through social media, be thankful for seeing that day and tell the universe exactly how you want your day to go, sparing no detail. Be honest with yourself. What do you want to eat for breakfast? What long awaited response to an important email would you like? Have you sold an item on your online store? Expect no traffic on a commute that's typically bumper to bumper, unless it's the 405 freeway in Los Angeles. I'm kidding! Seriously, setting your intention for your day before you get out of bed will lay out the roadmap for the universe to follow. However, the work doesn't stop there.

Many people fail at this step because the moment the slightest inconvenience occurs, they revert back to their old habits of thought. If you recall the previous chapter, this is that infamous "habit loop" we talked about. You have to truly believe in what you want and be prepared to receive it however the universe chooses to deliver it to you. Think of this as the midpoint. As a child, I believed my taste of stardom would come from being the biggest rap artist of my time. I thought I had to make it in music first and only then could I progress to television like my favorite hip-hop artists. The universe heard my intentions and delivered what I wanted at a time that I was best prepared to receive it, in a way that made me appreciate it one hundred times more. This increased my faith. What some people think is luck is actually a moment they've prepared for. It arrives at a time when their consistency, attitude and gratitude shows that they are ready to receive it.

Being aware of your thoughts, and immediately correcting yourself when you sway in a less-than-positive direction is the key to manifestation. You cannot trick the universe into delivering what you don't truly believe you can achieve. Replace the "I hope I can" with "I know I can" today and see the difference it makes in your day. Begin speaking of the things you want as if you already have them. For some, it may seem crazy, but you have to step into the shoes of who you want to be before you have fully transitioned to that state. Think of it as test driving your future self. You have to feel how you would feel, think how you would think, and behave how you would behave.

No day should pass that you aren't setting aside time to work on your goals. Don't forget, though visualizing the achievement is key, so is aligning yourself with that frequency through your work. Every moment you spend working on yourself and your goals should be given no less than 100 percent. It's easy to say what you would have done differently in retrospect, but when you walk in faith and intention you have to be aware of what you will do now because it directly affects your future.

I was great at creating routines I didn't follow and making promises to myself that I didn't keep and I know I'm not the only person with this talent. We've all said it: "New Year, New Me." As the fall months retreat and winter pokes its frosty head in, many people begin to think of their New Year resolutions. What's something I ignored all year that I absolutely must deal with in the new year? *This year is going to be my year.* It all starts off great and we're optimistic for what's to come. The problem is that for many, the world around influences us, and by mid-January we've already forgotten our resolutions and reverted back to the same behaviors we tried to leave behind the previous year.

Any positive change, big or small, will create a positive ripple in your journey so long as you remain consistent. For me, that first major physical change was the color of my hair. You may think *all you did was change your hair color, no big deal.* At that point in my life it was a big deal. Changing my hair color helped me gain new confidence as I was already working on strengthening my mental aptitude. I felt like a brand new person. Ultimately, it also helped me further develop my creative identity or the "persona" that I'd been searching for my entire life. I became a recognizable public figure. If you didn't know my name, you knew the hair and thus the *GreenHairedGirl* was born.

I was able to create an entire brand from this. My YouTube channel called *GreenHairedGirlVlogs* organically grew from a mere 92 subscribers and less than one thousand views to over ten thousand subscribers and two million views. This milestone took me just a year to reach, with much of the growth in the early months. I uploaded on a constant basis for only four months (Feb 2019 to Jun 2019) and built a following strong enough to push my analytics through the roof. So while I may not have been uploading for several months, YouTube still recommended my videos to new viewers because previous viewers continued to return and watch them. I also still engaged my following by responding to comments. I'm not saying this can happen for everybody as each of our journeys is different and you may very well have more exponential growth than I did, but the same key takeaway applies to all: *Make each stride count.*

Going back to the value of time, think about what you do on any typical day. What time do you wake up? If you work a nine to five, how much time do you spend in the bathroom getting ready? How much time is spent during your commute? What do you do when you get home? If you are working from home, do you spend your downtime fiddling through your social media or watching television? Have you ever picked up your phone without even realizing and opened your favorite app? How long can you actually keep your hands off of your phone? How much time in your day do you actually spend with yourself? No, I mean *really* with yourself?

Allowing your mind, body and soul its much needed regeneration period.

I've tried and failed many times at time management. I often had a laundry list of unimportant things to do before I could sit down and relax. Many times my partner would urge me to sit down, but I felt I had to do these things because the fate of the world depended on it. I wondered why I was so tired, busy and still unfulfilled. I didn't' figure it out until I'd had a serious chat with myself about what I was spending my time doing. I learned that being busy does not mean being productive and I would spend a hefty chunk of my time doing a bunch of things that did not align with the goals I had set for myself. What I was doing wasn't creating those positive ripples in my journey. I noticed that I would often pick up my phone and open my favorite social media apps, mindlessly scrolling through my feed. Soaking in like a sponge a wide array of "mental junk food" that satisfied a short-term craving, but had unhealthy long-term side effects when overconsumed. Social media was my puppeteer and I was strung to its mercy. One second, I was laughing at videos of dogs doing funny things, the next I was upset at injustices overwhelming my news feed and topping it all off with the latest celebrity gossip. This was a daily occurrence that was taking a toll on not only my mental health, but also my success because I allowed it to. I had to make a change and fast.

Every time I felt the urge to grab my phone, instead I picked up that book I'd been "reading" for two long months. I committed to finishing the chapter I was on. Another urge to pick up my phone? Time to delete the apps; out of sight—out of mind. Let's grab our journal and go over those long-term and short-term goals we wrote down several weeks ago. I slowly, but surely began to replace activities that undermined my goals with activities that were more valuable and I started to see the difference in what I began receiving from the universe. I didn't have to work harder, only smarter. It was unbelievable how much things began to change in the world around me. I started to see that each moment I spent on things that held value not only for myself, but also those around me, I was being rewarded for doing so. The amount of synchronicity that started to occur made me an even bigger believer in the Law of Attraction. I could spend my morning finishing a song project I'd been putting off and by the afternoon I had made several sales in the online store I created as an additional stream of income. It was as though the universe was saying to me, "Finally! I've been waiting to give this to you."

Take a moment to reflect on how your "free" time is spent. Ironically, free time is the most costly thing you spend. If you are employed, this might be before work, on your breaks or after, once you've set aside time for your responsibilities. If you're also a home-maker, this could be any amount of time you have outside of your routine. Based on whatever you do, you decide when this time is. Do you spend your time on personal development or personal vices? Only one of these ensures your growth. Do you find yourself turning on the television and escaping your own reality by watch-ing someone else's? We all know someone who just can't wait to tell you all of the latest drama on that popular TV show they watch religiously.

It's easy to become fully invested in something that gives us no returns. This may temporarily release those happy hormones, but what have you accomplished from it? Being on TV didn't make me watch more of it. In fact, I was probably one of the last people to catch my commercial on television. These days when a song I've written is placed on a TV show or film, I won't know it's aired until one of my business partners shares the news and only then will I watch the clip it's been played in and share it on social media to further promote my brand. It took a lot of discipline, but I was able to break the urges I had to frequent my social media apps. I knew I had to be particularly strict on myself.

Now I'm not saying bury yourself in your work and have no fun because too much of that is equally unhealthy, but moderation is key. Most people overwork themselves and burn out quickly or don't work hard enough to keep the flame alive. I believe that you can find a balance, but it will take a sacrifice to achieve this balance. If your goal is to make your passion your paycheck, anything that does not correlate with this goal can hit the road. If you want to lose or gain a few pounds then obviously you'll have to change your eating habits and exercise. If you want to learn another language, instead of opening your Instagram open a language app you can learn from on your phone. If you want to learn how to invest or trade, pick up a book, sign up for a course and practice reading charts on mobile investment apps instead of reading celebrity gossip or the latest conspiracy theories on *Reddit*.

When you create the habit of doing things that are working for you rather than against you, you won't miss the things you gave up to achieve that. As you grow, new opportunities and experiences will present themselves and fulfill you so that there is no longer a void to fill.

9

The Story of Me Part V

Since discovering my gift and passion for music at a young age my long-lived goal was to finally get a record deal, because to me, that was the ultimate ratification of success. I would look carefully at the industry and often mimic the things I saw signed artists doing. When that didn't work I began to brew my own formula of success. Every stage I could get on, you bet I did. Every artist that reached out to collaborate got their heart's desire. The industry began to change, and I, too, changed. It turned into a digital era of music and I loved every bit of it. Instead of bugging my grandmother or mom for a ride somewhere, I could showcase my talent on the world wide web to millions of people from the comfort of my living room. I took to learning a bit of marketing and promotions, photoshop, and even sales. After all, selling something doesn't always mean a physical product.

My name started to gain traction via the internet and when you searched for me on Google, I was the first result you'd see. This came with a perk and opened many doors. The very people I once wanted to access, now had direct access to me. All of this strategic work resulted in new opportunities. Some were lessons and others were blessings, but again, this is what I had asked the universe for before I knew how to be *intentionally specific*. Being intentionally specific is the act of asking for exactly what you want in detail and leaving nothing to question.

After many years of trial and error and building a solid following both online and offline I was finally signed to a boutique label. This was long before being on television, that helped bring my dreams to fruition. This was what all my hard work was for. I honestly don't recall planning beyond my signing day because that was always the dangling carrot.

In the beginning, I had stars in my eyes. It started as an amazing experience that I will credit for keeping me afloat, especially after the passing of my grandmother. I was fortunate enough to experience opportunities many dream of; I traveled the country, and met and picked the brains of some of the industry's best and brightest. I created lifelong bonds. However, after a while I could feel my flame burning out. The routine became robotic. The end goal became unclear, I was losing my love for it all and fast.

As I got more involved with the industry there were many things that occurred behind the scenes. Not all were bad, nor were all good. My label said one of my songs wasn't good enough and refused to take it on. I'd finally had enough and waited for my contract to end so that I could move forward with a new chapter. I recorded the song in my bedroom and released it myself. That song went on to become one of my most successful records to date, being played on the radio and even getting a stamp of approval by an industry gatekeeper. I was able to perform at multiple venues at the SXSW music festival in Austin, Texas and the song was also placed on Spotify's "Fresh Finds: Fire Emoji" playlist curated by their editors. I toured many high schools alongside Fresh Empire and Power 106 and performed that very record. The entire time that I had believed my success was at the mercy of someone else, my true success was always in my own hands.

For a long time I was convinced that I could do nothing without the label. In reality, before they stepped into the picture, I had been doing everything with just my small circle of friends who shared the same love for creation. No egos, no monetary gain, no politics. Just love for the art. I had been putting someone else in the driver's seat of my future, allowing them to pace my potential and growth. It was crippling. I was never destined to be anything less than a leader and in the forthcoming chapters we'll delve into the science behind it.

10

So, We Pivot

"Man plans, and God laughs."
—Yiddish Proverb

* * *

Sometimes, even if we plan it out, it doesn't go according to that plan and instead of feeling discouraged and sulking in self pity, you need to pivot. Think of a skilled boxer in the ring during one of the most important fights of his or her life. In most cases, when they're hit with a punch that doesn't result in a knockout, they calculate their next move and switch their stance, adapting to the new conditions; a.k.a. avoiding their opponent landing more critical punches.

I'm sure you've seen it in job listings: "Seeking a diligent worker able to adapt to a fast-paced work environment." This is exactly that! If you can "pivot" a.k.a. adapt and adjust to someone else's plan, you can and *must* do the same for yourself. When faced with adversity many throw their hands up and quit, but you cannot accept the same fate for yourself. The moment you even let the thought cross your mind, you're losing. Back to the rat race. This isn't the life I want for you and if you've made it this far, this isn't the life that you want for yourself. There should never be a question of *what if.* I'd rather tell an exhilarating story about what happened when I tried, failed, kept trying and succeeded versus wondering what could have happened if I'd never quit.

The fact that you are on a journey to attaining more knowledge is proof enough that you know what it takes to better your circumstances. The power is not in the amount of money you have, but the amount of knowledge you have. Money is merely a tool used to enhance your life experiences. It's in your hands. The tool will only be as useful as you can make it. Too often we've heard stories of celebrities or regular people that have suddenly been blessed with wealth. They lose it and end up worse than they started out. The real power is in what you know in the moment.

I once watched a thriller film where a young girl was being hunted down in the most remote area of the woods. She was injured and scared. One of her captors restrained her by tying a thick rope around her wrists. When he stepped outside for a moment she was left with no weapon, only knowledge. If someone doesn't look beyond what's in front of them, they won't see any tool available. They will be left with no choice but to resign themselves to their fate. The girl in the film, however, noticed a small metal bucket of sodium hydroxide lye in the form of flakes that she recalled her captor using earlier. With her knowledge, she knew that the water that he left within arms reach would force the lye to have a chemical reaction and produce a lot of heat. Armed with these items she poured the lye and water onto the rope, burning it. She was able to free herself. In this moment, her previous knowledge saved her life because if she had known no better, neither of those items would have mattered in the heat of the moment.

I've seen individuals with so much potential give in to less-than-favorable conditions because they could see no way out. This couldn't be more false. There is always a way out. You often hear these people speak more of the not-so-good into their life. They feed the problems in front of them, asking "Why me?" or saying "This always happens." This is a typical human response to anything negative. It causes confusion, frustration and even anger. By now we know enough to understand that as far as the universe is concerned you are asking for more of this. If it can be fixed, there's no need to worry. If it can't be fixed, there's no need to worry. Nature tends to appear chaotic at times, but if you look very closely at the chaos, you will always find traces of order. Trust the process.

The path to what we each consider our own success is one with many twists, turns and detours. If it were an easy journey you would hear stories of those closest to you reaching an immense success every single day, and it's likely you'd have reached your own by now. It is up to you and only you whether or not every single thing you wish to have or accomplish becomes your reality. If your goal is your true passion and purpose, then your "Plan B" should be nothing other than an alternate route to completion of your "Plan A". No matter what comes your way you must feel deep down that you will overcome it; it will not overcome you. In a sense, this is the most acceptable time to practice stubbornness, in your refusal to give up on yourself.

The route you choose to take in the heat of the moment will determine how the next sequence of events unfolds. Each action is dependent on another. If we're being mindful here, take a minute to think about an instance where your reaction to something seemingly negative led to a series of other events that caused you an even greater amount of grief. If you were mentally connected versus emotionally connected in that moment how could you have better navigated the situation to flip it, or pivot the odds in your favor? Or at the very least, soften the blow?

The ego plays a huge role in how we respond to the life that is always happening around us. We identify with our beliefs and if anyone appears to oppose those beliefs we try to one-up them. The ego offers us a false sense of victory if we succeed. Instead of trying to understand people who do and think differently to us we have an urge to get people to agree with us. This is especially pointless if the matters are more trivial than moral. We have a need to control and change the things around us to fit our narrative instead of changing ourselves. If you cannot find a common ground and you cannot live with the fact that this is the reality, let it go, because the work on yourself and your life still has to be done and you are the only person who can do it. We have to quit this belief of competition and replace it with creation. Don't compete for better, create it.

"Hurt people, hurt people," they say. When we feel that someone has made us upset the first thing we want to do is make them feel even more pain. What is this worth to you? Your future? Your happiness? Your inner peace? All this does is create a whirlpool of negative karmic energy that is surely best avoided.

The ego is the assassin of all potential. We've seen this on plenty of reality docuseries. A person on a path to greatness, who has overcome so much strife. They end up in a situation that gives them two choices; walk away or feed your ego. Boom! They lose it all in the blink of an eye. I speak from experience when I say it isn't worth it and it never will be. We know individuals like this. If only they had kept their wits about them, where would they be today? Staying and fighting doesn't make you stronger, and walking away doesn't make you weak.

Animals do not know egos, only natural order. There are entire ecosystems that are connected to this order and operate off of its energy. This order doesn't care if you're having a good or bad day, it will always do what it is designed to do. Why must you suffer a million times from temporary feelings instead of simply doing what you were designed to do, which is create? Create that television show you think will be a hit. Create the best version of yourself. Create your happiness. Yes! Create your happiness. Many people wait for happiness to be dropped into their lap, it doesn't work that way. Happiness isn't lost. Happiness is everywhere around you if you choose to see it in its natural state, which is in the form of energy.

All creation stems from a continuous flow of energy. What you focus your energy on, you create more of. When you are hungry and you decide to cook a meal because that will solve your issue of hunger, you are focusing your energy on the creation of that meal. You are the master of this creation. If you are a writer and have an idea of a book or script, or maybe even a song, the fate of this creation is up to you and only you. You are the designer of a bespoke creativity. And there is no better time than now to take advantage of the uniqueness that is you. It doesn't matter who came before nor who will come after you. There will never be another you. This is why no one but you has control over your present or future. I cannot feel for you. I cannot think for you. I cannot act on your behalf. I can merely give you the tools and let you focus your energy on what you choose to create.

I've shown how tough of a chick I can be many times. I've let my ego take the wheel in the heat of the moment and I gained nothing from it but a reputation for being someone you shouldn't mess with. However, I can't deposit that into the bank and I don't think it would look too great on my resume. This often led people to fear approaching me or avoiding me at all costs because they weren't sure how I would react. I created this.

I learned that I needed to be more proactive than reactive. When presented with problems, I began to approach them head on with solutions instead of doubt, anger, or worry. When I found myself under pressure I ensured I was mentally connected instead of emotionally reactive and when necessary, I found a balance between the two by being empathetic to the feelings of others. After all, who am I to tell someone the way I made them feel is not true? This gave me a split second, which is all it takes most cases, to be mindful of my response to whatever is happening. This practice alone has avoided me a lot of unnecessary grief and even repaired my reputation. People began to notice this change and put a new-found trust in my ability to bring about positive outcomes.

Life is like a game of chess. Though it is a competitive game, in reality you are actually *creating* a way for your pieces to cross-over to the opposite end of the board. When you know every move you make may cost you, you practice some caution and mindfulness before you make your next move. You take the time to think of strategic ways to advance yourself, often several steps ahead. This process excites you and thinking of the results makes you happy. If you can do this with a simple board and game pieces that can easily be replaced as many times as you wish, why not treat your life, which is the only one you have to live, with the same heedful handling and intent?

11

The Story of Me Part VI

All while I chased my dreams of musical stardom and even while on television I held an hourly position at one of the most successful, new (at the time), technology companies in the world. I was fortunate enough to work this job with not one, but several very supportive supervisors throughout my tenure. They allowed me time away from work to go to the studio, auditions and rehearsals because, even though it was against the greater good of the job, they believed in my gift and knew I was destined for more. They allowed me to be me. This was only the second job I'd ever held.

After enjoying the successes I'd seen from music and television, I decided it was time to take a break and recalibrate myself. I felt I'd done everything I could in that particular season and needed some time to live a more humble lifestyle and figure out the transition to my next chapter. With that in mind, I took another hiatus from entertainment and focused on my nine to five employment. Bills still needed to be paid. Although when the music and TV paid, it paid handsomely, it wasn't a consistent-enough cash-flow.

For many creatives, or maybe it's just a me thing, being told what to do, when to do it and how to do it isn't something that's easy getting used to. To go from having production assistants waiting on me hand and foot, being able to create whatever I wanted, when I wanted, to being yelled at and threatened by upset consumers and meeting deadlines for a company whose CEO only saw me as a metric was a huge culture shock for me. *No one speaks to me that way. Who do these people think they are? Do they not know who I am?* I loathed every moment of dealing with unruly customers and unrealistic expectations and made sure they all knew it. I carried a chip on my shoulder. But at the end of the day, I chose to be there. I could quit at any moment, but I knew I had to stick to my guns and tough it out for the sake of my livelihood.

I constantly found myself in some type of trouble at work, but my saving grace was the fact that I knew how to do my job exceptionally well (minus taking the customer's crap), and like "Little Me" I could talk my way out of almost anything. There was still a light and magnetism about me that drew people near and I forged heartfelt bonds with most of my colleagues. Many have become like my extended family.

I was very headstrong and mordacious and by now, everyone knew it was "just how I was", but that didn't make it any less wrong. I was on a very low vibration and my environment was responding to that with more sequences that kept me vibrating low. I recall applying for a senior support expert position at the next level, not once, but three times. This position would give me more responsibility and authority at the job and even my own office space. The first time was to get my feet wet––of course I wasn't prepared for it, but I was very cocky anyway. The second time, I truly felt as though I deserved the role. However, though I worked harder, I wasn't working smarter and the frequencies I put out were still less than favorable. After that second time I decided I would never apply for that role again and was surely planning my exit.

My supervisor had a heart to heart with me. It wasn't a boss and their employee talking, it was two human beings having a real conversation. She spoke to me about how I had improved since the first time I applied for the role, but there were still a few things I needed to work on. It didn't matter what anyone told me though. It wasn't until I came to my own realization and acceptance that I knew what I needed to do next. I thought my way of doing things was the end all, be all, but it was time to pivot. And pivot I did. I unpacked the baggage I couldn't take with me to this next chapter and showed my colleagues, and most importantly, the universe, that I was prepared to receive whatever was coming to me. Oddly enough, a third opening was created for the very position I sought, even though in the past there had only ever been two people in that role. This time around I *knew* in my heart it was mine and my work spoke for me.

I applied for the job and nailed my presentation and interview. Within a few days I was notified that I had received the role and was given my offer letter. The whole process taught me a great deal about humility, but also the importance of packing for the journey. This was the beginning of what would be a steady ascent during my tenure with this company. I took my newfound responsibility very seriously. Taking the initiative to do things others would not do, I created solutions that equated order instead of more chaos. I worked with colleagues to find ways to not only be more customer-forward, but also bring some of the fun back to the office. I was content in my role and had no thoughts about what was next for me until the people around me began to groom me for the next level.

About seven months into my new role, a higher-level managerial position opened and it was without a doubt that I was ready to receive it. Initially I wanted nothing to do with the added stress of being what I called the "big boss", but the increase in both power and pay was pretty tempting. I decided to get out of my head and go for it. And I'm glad I did. The same girl who started out at ground zero, always in some sort of trouble and set in her ways, made some simple, but much-needed changes to herself which ultimately changed her circumstances. I now had the power to create the workplace environment of my dreams. To cultivate my team of gifted support experts and, even if it is beyond the job, to mentor them to discover the things they are great at.

I made it a point to always be honest, transparent and available for my team. Reminiscent of my previous managers, my goal was not merely to make sure a job was done right, but support my people in such a way that they wanted to do the job right in support of me. Life is full of cycles and this was a part of that. When you feel great, you do great. What you give, you will always receive back.

A few months passed and lo and behold! An even higher position of power was created. The holder of this role would not only be responsible for my team of experts, but also multiple facilities, vendors and stakeholders. Many shots would have to be called and the role-holder would be the one to call them. Remember what I said about preparing to receive? Without knowing this opportunity would arise, I was already doing much of what was required at this next level on my own accord. You guessed it, after a lengthy interview process, and many worthy applicants across the country, I received my offer letter.

According to numerology, my life path is a "1". My significant other, who is a lot better versed in numerology than I, explains this is why all roads in my life, no matter how tough they've been to navigate, have taken me to a point where I had to step up and take charge. I often wondered why people always came to me for insight or my opinion on matters that didn't concern me no matter their age, or how my grandmother somehow knew I would be best suited to take care of things when her time came. I wanted it to stop and it never did. This was the natural order of who I was destined to become: a leader.

Some of the favorable characteristics of someone with a 1 life path is independent, self-motivated, innovative, compelling, trustworthy and compassionate to name a few. Adversely, some of the less-than-favorable characteristics can be aggressive, defensive, and egoistic behavior. I thought I could make the bad traits disappear by building upon the good, but at the end of it all I was just a really skilled individual that was still an asshole. I had to look in the mirror and check myself before I could see any real improvement.

We all eventually find ourselves in that pivotal moment where we can either continue to do what we know does us no good (and get the same results), or face the "ugly" head on and rid ourselves of it forever. This will open the doors to a life of great possibility. I didn't realize how scary it must have been for others to face me at my worst until I decided to face myself. Which version of you will come out victorious?

12

Pack for the Journey

"We all have baggage, but there comes a time when you
realize it's time to unpack."
—Unknown

* * *

Take only what you need and nothing more—think of this as
packing for your journey to whatever you consider your success.
Think of all the good things you want to place in your luggage.
Remove any heavy, negative items or habits that may weigh you
down or hinder you. Leave negative thoughts and self doubt at bay.
Pack prosperity and optimism. Make room for self-love and confidence. You can never have too much gratitude. There's more than
enough room for that.

Each time you complete a long or short-term goal or reach a
milestone, unpack what you no longer need and add what you feel
will suit you best for the next phase of your journey. "Your life does
not get better by chance, it gets better by change." —Jim Rohn

You must genuinely give your all in order to receive it all. This will be a trying journey. All things that are good are under constant attack, but it is your responsibility to build a fortress that no Trojan horse can penetrate. Remain steadfast in what you want for yourself and those that you love.

The surest, and most successful form of packing for one's journey is the act of self-reflection. Self-reflection is the process of unplugging from the world and introspecting your thoughts, behaviors, priorities and motives. We find it so easy to watch and critique others and their actions. We often give unsolicited opinions or feedback that we don't even live by. There goes that ego again. What happens when we place ourselves under that same critical microscope? Being self-aware is not something you should fear. It is one of the most liberating experiences we can encounter as humans. Think of it as looking left, right, and left again before crossing a busy street.

Self-reflection is an attribute of some of the world's most successful people. If you don't believe me, ask Oprah Winfrey. This isn't something you can do for a day and expect everything to change. The first day is a great start, but you have to commit to completing this act on a regular basis.

This "soul-searching" is critical to all areas of success in your life, be it business or pleasure. The outcome is that you're provided with a different perspective. In a way it's like Google Maps where you're able to zoom out and see beyond your point of interest. It allows you to assess certain situations in the past where you may have reacted in a less than pleasant manner. Though it will not take back anything you may have said or done, it will allow you to proceed more thoughtfully should a similar occurrence present itself in the future. It helps you peel back layers and reach the core of what makes you tick.

I know you're wondering, *Jess, how do I practice self-reflection?* I promise the process isn't as painful as it seems. It can be broken into two parts: you, and the areas in life that you find most important. I recommend grabbing a journal or some paper and a pen. You can also use the notes app on your phone. You want to keep this notebook as your archive, or record of reflection. I always find it easier to gather, outline and process my thoughts when I am able to write them down. It makes things more palpable and gives you the perspective to then determine how to improve it or let it go entirely.

Find a quiet area in your home. If you're tight on space you can always drown out the world using headphones and music with no words. I personally listen to binaural beats that produce certain Solfeggio frequencies. These are specific tones of sound that promote health of the mind and body.

Once you are in a comfortable space it's time to be vulnerable with yourself. Think of a situation, either today or in the past, where you have found yourself in a situation that you could have responded to differently. Identify how you could have responded better and how that response could have brought about a more pleasant series of events. Were you in your head too much when you could have been more emotionally available? Or were you too emotional when you should have been more logical? Now is not the time to be a harsh judge on yourself. Look at the events with an unbiased eye. You are now a third party to the situation. We are only using introspection to understand why you responded how you did and what could have been done differently. When you disarm your ego, what answers do you hear coming from within? What are the steps you will take moving forward to improve or change?

The act of self-reflection can go as deep within as you will allow it. You can uncover your beliefs and values, skills and talents, strengths and weaknesses. Think about how you want to contribute and add value to the people and things around you. Reflect on your finances, your relationships with family, friends, or significant others. Your health, career, personal development and attitude. What do you want in these areas? What's working and what's not? What can you improve? Asking yourself these simple questions will uncover a lot of new truths for you. These truths are not here to harm you, but to set you free.

So what is the price of your freedom? According to American author Elbert Hubbard, it is responsibility. I believe it is taking responsibility for one's actions. Being mindful of all that you put into the universe and being grateful for what you receive. If you don't like what you receive, remove anything that attracts more of it. You know the drill. Everything you do, everything you feel is like a magnet. William Ernest Henley once wrote, "I am the master of my fate, the captain of my soul." We are masters. We are creators of infinite realms of possibility. We are bearers of so much potential and power as long as we believe. Ha. It's that simple. Belief. Faith. Unwavering fortitude in our life's journey. YOU are the key to life.

Epilogue

THE FIRST STEP

Thank you. Thank you. Thank you for taking the first step in moving towards all things good for you. Thank you for hearing my story. Thank you for believing in yourself. Thank you for loving yourself. Thank you in advance for all of the greatness you will create.

I wrote this book with an open mind and a pure heart. At times, it wasn't an easy task and I sometimes let my own doubt seep in and fool me into thinking this was a silly idea. While sharing my experiences and life lessons with you, I, too, uncovered so much more about myself that I never knew. I learned about areas I can continue to work to improve. I learned about special skills and strengths I may have overlooked. I peeled back a lot of layers I forgot about. I laughed about it. I cried about it. I felt hopeful and rejuvenated. I forgave myself as well as others. This was a moment of liberation for me and I hope you share in that liberty.

When you find yourself in the midst of your full circle moment, the moment where your purpose and what must be done to fulfill it is as clear as the waters surrounding Oceania, you will experience such a feeling of warmth and completion. But that is only the beginning of your journey. As you uncover more of your truth and build upon the things that add value to your life you will be tasked with a great responsibility. That responsibility is not only about being prepared to receive, but also being gracious enough to give with no expectation of return. And when you serve others, it cannot be with a stingy heart or out of some insincere intent or to gain approval. The universe will not fall for such trickery. You have what someone else in this world needs. And when the stars are aligned and your paths cross, giving it to them will never leave you with less than what you need to keep thriving.

You have to be willing to be vulnerable with yourself. It's our natural defense mechanism to keep a wall up that no one can penetrate, not even ourselves. This sets us back and keeps us confined in a bubble. We remain pacified by a series of beliefs that have been passed down that we feel are the law. They are not. They are no one's law, not even yours. You chose none of what you were born with, not even your name. Now you have the freedom to choose. You can choose to continue on the path you are on now or take the first step in a new direction. A direction where you will flourish and blessings will overflow. A direction where your intentions are clear and meaningful. A direction where it is not just about you, but all of the life you touch.

I wish you peace. I wish you good health. I wish you wealth. I wish you inspiration. I wish you happiness. I wish you love. I wish you a higher consciousness. I wish you strength and determination. However, I will not wish you luck. You don't need it.

I look forward to seeing what you create.

Acknowledgements

It's easier to say you want to write a book than it is to wake up one day and commit to actually writing one. It's hard to share pieces of my life that many close to me may not have known until now. To let total strangers, who I hope now see me as extended family after reading this, into my mind and heart. To share my magic and experiences in hopes of sparking the flame within each of you. This is not something that I could have done alone. Each of the following people have played a part in the creation of this book whether they know it or not.

To my parents, Yolanda and Michael, thank you for going half on me. Mom, I know I wasn't the easiest child to raise, especially as I began to form opinions of my own, but I thank you for working countless hours and multiple jobs to provide for us. I may act nonchalant at times, but every moment we spend on the phone or together I truly cherish. Whether you're making me laugh, work, or roll my eyes, know that I love you with my entire being. Dad, I forgive you for everything. I know you still feel remorse about not being around, but you've been the father I needed since our paths crossed again and I appreciate everything you've done for me. Meeting you has helped me make a lot of sense about who I am.

To my wife and partner in life, Lilliana, I know I'm a handful and I thank you for keeping me motivated to be the best version of myself. For introducing a new look at life and helping me find love for it all again. Thank you for stopping whatever you were doing to run over to my desk and read pieces of this book. Thank you for being honest in your feedback. Thank you for keeping me fed because we all know when I'm "in the zone" I forget to eat. I love you and owe you the world.

To whom I consider my best friend, Charles. We've been friends for what feels like a lifetime. Through it all you've shown me true friendship and taught me that there are people that exist that genuinely just want the best for others and nothing in return. Thanks for having my back.

The good people at Rescue Agency and Fresh Empire. I appreciate you all taking a chance on a green-haired girl from South Central. The opportunity I had to not only share my story, but inspire young kids from different backgrounds is something I will never forget. It was this experience that taught me nothing you want and work for is too far to reach.

To all of my wise, beautiful aunties. Thank you for stepping in and being there for me following the loss of our diva. Your love and words of encouragement kept me reminded that none of my work was in vain.

To anyone that I've ever interacted with beyond the surface. Thank you for the positive energy, the well wishes, the laughter we've shared, the unconditional support, and the bread we've broken together. There are so many of you, too many to name. This is for you. Thank you, thank you, thank you!

Jess Williams, an electrifying wordsmith and music virtuoso, emerged from the bustling streets of South Central, Los Angeles, where she absorbed the wisdom passed down by her grandmother and mother. Guided by an insatiable curiosity, she uncovered the inner workings of the world, setting her sights on a destiny intertwined with writing and music—a passion that flowed through her veins.

As she pursued her musical dreams, Williams embarked on a profound journey of self-discovery, delving into the intricate realm of the Law of Attraction. Armed with this transformative knowledge, she propelled herself to extraordinary heights, ultimately becoming the face of a groundbreaking national FDA campaign targeting multicultural youth. Her captivating presence radiated across screens, airwaves, glossy magazines, and towering billboards, leaving an indelible mark on countless hearts.

Harnessing the boundless wellspring of her potential, Williams seized the countless opportunities that followed her meteoric rise. Now, in her highly anticipated second book, "No One's Loser," she offers a compelling exploration of manifestation, guiding readers to manifest the life of their dreams. With a captivating blend of personal anecdotes, practical wisdom, and a modern sensibility, Williams connects with readers on a profound level, empowering them to rise above limitations and embrace their true potential.

Prepare to be captivated and enlightened as Jess Williams shares her extraordinary journey, unraveling the secrets that will enable you to manifest the life of your dreams. Within the pages of "No One's Loser," she invites you to challenge the notion of failure, inspiring you to create your own reality and become the architect of your destiny. With her magnetic prose as your guide, you'll embark on an exhilarating quest of self-discovery, empowered to overcome obstacles and transform setbacks into stepping stones on your path to success.

Milton Keynes UK
Ingram Content Group UK Ltd.
UKHW020733161023
430697UK00016B/735